Sandra Williams is a practicing speech-language pathologist certified by the American Speech-Language-Hearing Association (ASHA). She has worked with children and adults in a v̶ ̶ ̶ ̶ ̶ ̶ ̶ ̶ ̶ ̶ in the areas of articulation, language, voice, fluency ar

Parent Testimor

"Ms. Williams was very warm, welcoming, and loving. My daughter surprisingly opened up to her instantly… and started to acquire more words and use them correctly. My daughter became more social and even her teachers said they had seen an improvement. Ms. Williams has been a godsent to our family and we are all appreciative." - L. Barrington

"I truly believe that each time Sandra sits down for a session she gives the client a piece of her. Thank you Sandra for being one of the individuals that I attribute to my daughter's ongoing progress. I think you are an awesome person." - Lorena Chavis

"Ms. Sandra Williams is truly a godsent. Her ability to verbally guide a nonverbal child to use his/her voice to make requests and express themselves is amazing. We can see Ms. Williams' passion for working with children in her patience and care for our son. I never thought I would hear my son's voice and within a couple of months Ms. Williams changed that for us. We are eternally grateful to have her in our son's life." - Kim Jackson

"Sandra is both very clinically experienced and talented as well as very warm and caring. She takes a holistic approach in her play-based therapy practice with a holistic focus on the well-being of your child. My son loved working with Sandra and made tremendous progress with his expressive language skills and articulation during his time working with her!" - Liz Warner, MBA and parent of two

"Ms. Sandra came to us at a time of a complete whirlwind of emotions. She very quickly made us feel safe and at ease with the long road ahead of us. As a family, we were uncertain as to how this would work. The kids took to her immediately. She had daily drills and exercises that she used to help develop their skills. She advised us on exercises to try on our own. Ms. Sandra became more than just a speech therapist for our family. She became a counselor, a teacher, and most importantly a friend. Our kids have grown so much due to working with her. THANK YOU Ms. Sandra. Our family was blessed to have you walk into our lives." - Kevin Wilson

Lullabelle & Friends' PARENT GUIDE

Enhancing Your Child's Speech-Language Development From Birth to Three Years and Beyond...

Sandra Fay Williams, MS, CCC-SLP
Illustrated by EmilyAnn Bamfield

Lullabelle & Friends' Parent Guide
Enhancing your Child's Speech-Language Development
From Birth to Three Years and Beyond...

Copyright © 2020 by Sandra Fay Williams, MS, CCC-SLP

Disclaimer: This book is presented solely for educational purposes and does not constitute medical advice; nor is it a substitute or replacement for health professional advice, diagnosis or treatment.

Ordering information contact:
www.Parentspeechguide.com

ISBN 978-1-7340472-0-2

To John Anthony Williams

Hi, my name is Lullabelle!
My friends, Gabriel, Sydney, Matt and I are all newborns
on our way home to live with our brand new families.
Hola Gabriel! Hello Sydney! Konnichiwa Matt!
Our families are very different from each other. We look different.
We have different members and each of us has our own unique
customs. Nonetheless, we have outlined special tips that we are
asking **ALL** Mommies and Daddies to try that will help us become
really good talkers and really good listeners! These are fun ideas
that can be included into everyday activities to build up our
language skills.
Thank you for your cooperation in **ADVANCE**!

***The list of activities described in this guide is by no means all
that can be done to enhance your child's communication skills.
We have provided some terrific suggestions that will get you off to
a great start! If you have concerns regarding your child's
speech-language development, please talk with your pediatrician,
your local department of health or a licensed speech-language
pathologist.

****Make sure that the toys you purchase for your child are
age-appropriate. The suggested age-range on the packaging is a
very helpful guide.

Lullabelle: It's been three weeks since I arrived at my new home! I'm still a little scared. It's not as warm and cozy as my last home, but I'm sure I'll grow to love it here.

Surround your child with colorful toys and pictures. In the months ahead, she will be very interested in all that she sees around her.

Lulllabelle: Oops! I see that Gabriel is having some trouble!
Oooh! Aaah, that's much better.
Gabriel likes it when his Mommy holds him
and strokes his face.

Gabriel's Mom: Gabriel, what's the matter? Mommy's here.

Touching and talking
to your baby lovingly calms him
down and helps you to bond.
Enjoy these precious moments.

Lullabelle: Sydney's Dad does a great job caring for her.
He sings to her all the time. She loves his deep voice.
It makes her feel all gooey inside. Da, da, da...

Dad: Mary had a little lamb,
little lamb, little lamb...

Sing to your child regularly.
Music is a great way to
connect with your baby.

Giving your child face-to-face time is fun for her and for you!

Lullabelle: Now that Sydney is 4 months old, she loves to look into her Daddy's face. She sees his thick eyebrows, his big smile and his fuzzy hair.

Dad: Hi Sydney. How are you this morning?

Lullabelle: Matt does not always look at his Mom when she is talking or making sounds. That's why she plays games with him and shows him bold, brightly colored toys. If she keeps doing that, I think Matt will begin to look at her more and more.

Matt's Mom: The Itsy Bitsy Spider went up the waterspout...

Some babies may not look at you directly. Parents can use colorful toys and noisemakers to get their child's attention. See if they can follow the toy with their eyes.

Lullabelle: Mommy is always talking to me, even though she knows I don't understand a word she's saying.

Talk to your baby as you go about your day. She will love the sound of your voice.

Mom: I'm going to change your diaper and then we're going outside to see the pretty flowers at the park.

Lullabelle: After turning 4 months, I just babble away. I am figuring out all the different sounds I can make. "Ba, ba, ba, ba, da, da, da."

Lullabelle: Da, Da, Ba, Ba, Ba
Mommy: Whoa! Whee! Whooosh!
You like the bubbles? Let's make some more.
Oh, I see the big, shiny bubble. Pop! Pop!
Lullabelle: Hee, hee, hee!

It's okay to answer with words as your child is discovering new sounds. Go on! Have FUN!

Lullabelle: Look, Matt's Mommy talks to him even though he is not babbling or making sounds. She knows that when she talks to him, he is still listening. And one day he may be able to make those sounds, too.

Mom: I see that you are really hungry! After you eat, it's time for a nice long nap.

Talk and sing to your child even if he is not making sounds.

Mom: Once upon a time...

Lullabelle: Even though we're only 6 months old, our
Mommies and Daddies read to us every day.
Well, actually they've been reading to us since
day one! Can you believe that? I'm sure all of these
books will make us very smart.

Read to your baby daily.
She will enjoy the colorful pictures
and the funny sounds she hears
from you.

Lullabelle: Our Mommies and Daddies play with us **ALL** the time.
They understand that there is nothing more important
than **ONE-ON-ONE TIME** with them.
Look, I think they're having more fun than we are!

Gabriel's Mom: Yikes! Your red car is having engine trouble.
We have to get it fixed!

Play with your child by using interesting toys,
singing familiar nursery songs,
or engaging in fun finger-plays.
"Peek-a-boo," "Pat-a-cake," "The Wheels on the Bus"
are all childhood favorites. There is nothing like a
make-believe tea party or a made-up adventure hunt
as your child gets older.

11

Mom: Oh Matt, see the black and white zebra!
Looks like he's resting.

Lullabelle: Our Moms and Dads take us to lots of interesting
places—the park, the zoo, the grocery store and the
library, and it doesn't cost a dime! They always tell us
about the people and things we see.

Mom: I see that you are holding your favorite red and yellow blocks, Matt. I think we can stack them up!

Lullabelle: Now that it's been 18 months since our arrival, our Mommies and Daddies want us to begin to really concentrate on things. Sometimes we play games, like stacking blocks or putting objects in a box and dumping them out to see how long we can play before we want to do something different. Look! Matt likes blocks. His Mom will help him stack them up to make a tall tower.

Name objects and actions during your child's play. Help him concentrate to build tall towers or to take objects out of a container.

When you add to your child's
single words or short phrases,
you're providing them examples of
sentences they will try to say
in the future.

Lullabelle: Now that I can say some words, Mommy always adds to
what she thinks I am trying to say to make my
sentences longer.

Lullabelle: Out-side...
Mom: Yes, it's time to go outside to see the pretty flowers that are
blooming, because it's spring!
Lullabelle: Mommy is so smart. How does she know that that's what
I am thinking? Hmmmmmm.

Lullabelle: Matt's Mommy continues to talk to him using long and short sentences, even though he's not saying words. Matt sure is a good listener.

Mom: I am washing your face, Matt.
I see your beautiful round cheeks.

Even if your child is not saying words or making sounds, talk to him and explain what is happening. See if he changes his body or looks at you when you are speaking. Say out loud what you think your child might be feeling.

Lullabelle: When Mommy is fixing my cereal, or getting me ready for bed, she always tells me what she is doing. She knows that one day I will be big enough to do it by myself and she wants me to do a good job.

Mom: I'm going to pour your cereal into a bowl. Oh, we can't forget to pour in the milk.

Help your child understand how jobs are done such as, getting ready for bedtime or preparing a bowl of cereal. One day, they will want to try it all by themselves.

Daddy: This strawberry ice cream is soooo delicious!

Lullabelle: Not only does Sydney's Dad use little words, he also uses big words, like "delicious" and "scrumptious." At first, she does not know what these words mean. Her dad says "delicious" and "scrumptious" every time she eats her favorite strawberry ice cream. Sydney figures out that these big words mean that her ice cream tastes really "good."

Yayyyy! I think Sydney's brain is growing.

17

Lullabelle: Now that I am 2 years old, a lot of wonderful things are happening. Mommy is beginning to let me make choices. She will show me two things to eat - a banana and an apple - and she asks, "Which one do you want: the banana or the apple?" Before I had words, I would point. But now that I have my words, sometimes I say, "banana" and sometimes I say, "apple." It just depends on my mood. Hee-hee-hee!

Allowing your child to make choices will help increase confidence in their ability to make decisions.

Mom: That's a great choice, Lullabelle. I see you chose the shiny, red apple. Let's taste it to see if it's juicy and sweet.

Lullabelle: After you turn 2 years old, you have a lot of responsibilities. Gabriel's Mommy gives him jobs to do around the house. Sometimes, she has to tell him twice and show him, but she always lets him do it by himself. Although, it's OK if he needs a little help every now and then. His Mommy and Daddy will be happy to assist.

Mom: Gabriel, I like how you followed my directions. You put your favorite cup on the table and got your new green sneakers. Yay!!!

Give your child directions to complete simple jobs at home. Let him show you that he is a good listener.

Lullabelle: Matt's Mom has decided to seek services from a speech therapist to see if he needs a little help to make more sounds and say words. In the meantime, she knows that Matt is a big boy and she wants him to follow directions, too. So, his Mom asks, "May I have the toy car, please?" Matt gives it to her. Way to go Matt!

Mom: Thanks for giving me your favorite wooden car.

Lullabelle: When we go outside, Mommy allows me to explore my
surroundings and she names all the new things I see.
Mommy is soooo patient.

Foster new learning
by encouraging your child to
explore her
surroundings safely.

Mom: These flowers tickle your fingers.
They smell like sweet perfume.

Mom: Let's touch the pretty petals. I like the way they feel.

Lullabelle: Matt's Mom knows that he wants to touch the pretty
flower. So she helps him to reach out his hand and feel
the soft petals. Matt is smiling. I think he likes it!

Ask your child "open-ended" questions such as, "Where did you put your jacket?" rather than, "Is your jacket on the chair?" This will help them string words together to make longer sentences.

Mom: Why do you think that fire truck's siren is making that loud sound?

Lullabelle: Gabriel is two and a half, almost three years old, and his Mommy asks him a lot of questions that encourage him to use more words. Sometimes, I think that he is teaching her, not the other way around!

Lullabelle: Matt is not saying words. So his Mom asks him a bunch of questions that he can answer with "Yes" or "No." Look! Matt nods his head "Yes" to creamy, chocolate ice cream.

Mom: Do you want the ice cream?

If your child is not putting words together, ask "Yes" and "No" types of questions. You can add words to his answers. For example, "Yes, I see you want the chocolate ice cream."

Lullabelle: I also have a lot of questions that need answering like, "Where is the birdie going?" My Mommy tries to answer my questions. Sometimes, she smiles before answering. I wonder what she is thinking?

Mom: The birdie may be going to get little sticks to make a nest, or maybe she's going to look for food for her babies.

By answering your child's questions, you are improving their understanding.

Mom: You want to know
what that is called?
It's a nest. It's where
birdies live.

Lullabelle: Matt is pointing and making sounds. His Mommy figures
out that he wants to ask her about the birdie. And do
you know how she does this? She notices where his eyes
are focused, the sounds he makes, and how he uses his
body to gesture. Then she asks the question for him and
answers it, too! Wow, his Mommy is doing **Double Duty**!
Way to go Mom!

Mom: Now, we are going to go shopping at the grocery store to get your favorite fruits—bananas and apples!

To put your child at ease, explain what will happen next as you go about your day.

Lullabelle: When I am about to do something new that I have never done before, or when we are just changing from one activity to another, Mommy always tells me what to expect. She knows that I am very curious and that this information helps me to understand what I might see or experience.

Lullabelle: Oh, I see that Matt is crying because he is going to a new daycare. His Mommy lets him hold onto his favorite teddy bear and she shows him a picture of the new daycare before they arrive. I know that Matt will feel better soon.

Find ways to reassure your child when they are experiencing something new. A favorite toy and some comforting words may just do the trick.

As your child is learning about all the wonderful things around them, they will want to experiment to see how all of these things work. They may make a few mistakes. This is all a part of learning. Gently show them a different way to make new discoveries.

Mom: Lullabelle, we have to be careful when we go into the bathroom. We want to use drawing paper and crayons for our art projects, not toilet paper. Let's clean up first and afterwards we can color our masterpiece.

Lullabelle: Wow, being a toddler is so exciting! I am doing so many things for the first time. I'm glad that Mommy lets me make mistakes and gently shows me a better way. That makes learning a lot fun!

Lullabellle: Wow, we made it! We turned 3 years old!
We have had a great life so far and a very looooong day!
Whew, it's time for bed and to have our Mommies and
Daddies kiss us and tell us how much they love us.

"WE LOVE YOU TOO!"

Enjoy this wonderful time in your life
and in the life of your child. Treating them
lovingly during these early days and months will
set the stage for a bright future!

ADVICE FROM LULLABELLE, GABRIEL, SYDNEY AND MATT
BABIES LOVE IT WHEN YOU:

1. HOLD AND CUDDLE US.

2. LOOK AT US FACE TO FACE. WE LIKE LOOKING INTO YOUR EYES.

3. TALK TO US WHEN WE MAKE SOUNDS, OR EVEN WHEN WE ARE COMPLETELY SILENT. WE LOVE TO HEAR YOUR VOICE.

4. READ TO US DAILY. THERE'S NOTHING LIKE A GOOD BOOK.

5. SING TO US. WE LOVE MOVING OUR BODIES TO MUSIC.

6. JOIN US DURING FLOOR PLAY. YOU ARE OUR FIRST OFFICIAL PLAYMATES.

7. PLAY GAMES WITH US THAT HELP BUILD OUR CONCENTRATION, SUCH AS STACKING BLOCKS OR CONSTRUCTING PUZZLES. WE'RE GOING TO NEED IT.

8. TAKE US TO DIFFERENT PLACES AROUND THE COMMUNITY. WE LOVE GETTING OUT OF THE HOUSE TO LEARN NEW THINGS.

9. WHEN WE START TALKING, ADD WORDS TO WHAT WE SAY TO MAKE OUR SENTENCES LONGER.

10. EXPLAIN HOW YOU DO YOUR DAILY TASKS. WE WILL WANT TO TRY IT, TOO.

11. DURING OUR DAILY ROUTINE, SAY NEW WORDS WE MAY NOT KNOW. WE WILL BEGIN TO FIGURE OUT WHAT THEY MEAN.

12. ASK US QUESTIONS TO HELP US PRACTICE USING OUR WORDS AND GIVE US OPPORTUNITIES TO MAKE LOTS OF CHOICES.

13. ANSWER OUR QUESTIONS. WE ARE VERY CURIOUS.

14. AS WE GET OLDER, GIVE US "JOBS" TO DO AT HOME, SUCH AS SORTING OUR CLOTHES OR PUTTING AWAY OUR TOYS. WE WANT TO PROVE THAT WE CAN FOLLOW YOUR DIRECTIONS.

15. HELP US EXPLORE OUR SURROUNDINGS, SAFELY.

16. PLEASE PREPARE US WHEN WE ARE GETTING READY TO TRY SOMETHING NEW.

17. WHEN WE MAKE MISTAKES, WHICH IS A NATURAL PART OF LEARNING, GENTLY SHOW US A BETTER WAY TO DO THINGS.

18. PLEASE, ALWAYS LET US KNOW THAT YOU LOVE US! WE NEVER GET TIRED OF HEARING THOSE WORDS.

References

1. Baumwell L., Tamis-LeMonda C.S., (1997).
   Maternal verbal sensitivity and child language comprehension.
   Infant Behavior and Development, 20(2) 247-258.

2. Bornstein, M.H. (1985). How infant and mother jointly contributes to Developing cognitive competence in the child. Proceedings of the National Academy of Sciences, 82, 7470-7473.

3. Bornstein, M.H., & Benasich, A. A. (1986). Infant habituation: Assessments of short-term reliability and individual differences at 5 months.
   Child Development, 57, 87-99.

4. Bright Futures: Guidelines for Health Supervision of Infants, Children, and Adolescents, Third Edition, edited by Joseph Hagan, Jr., Judith S. Shaw, and Paula M. Duncan, 2008, Elk Grove Village, IL: American Acade my of Pediatrics.

5. Cates, C. et al. "Early Reading Matters: Long-term impacts of shared Bookreading with infants and toddlers on language and literacy outcomes." Presented at: The Pediatric Academic Societies Meeting: May 6-9, 2017; San Francisco, CA. Retrieved October 8, 2017 from http://www.aappublications.org/news/2017/05/04/PASLiteracy050417

6. Caring for your Baby and Young Child: Birth to Age 5, Fifth Edition edited by Steven Shelov and Tanya Remer Altmann © 1001, 1993, 1998, 2004, 2009 by American Acade my of Pediatrics.

7. Flippin, M., Watson L.R. Fathers' and mothers' verbal responsiveness and the language skills of young children with autism spectrum disorder. American Journal Speech-Language Pathology, 24, 400-410.

8. Infant Vision: Birth to 24 Months of Age: Steps in Infant Vision Development American Optometric Association. Retrieved October 9, 2017 from https://www.aoa.org/patients-and-public/good-vision-throughout-life/childrens-vision/infant-vision-birth-to-24-months-of-age#1

9. Menache, A., Atzaba-Poria, N., (2016).
   Parent-child interaction: Does parental language matter?
   British Journal of Development Psychology, 34, 518-537.

10. Roberts, M. Y., Kaiser, A. P., (2011).
    The effectiveness of parent-implemented language intervention: A meta-analysis.
    American Journal of Speech-Language Pathology, Vol. 20, 180-199.

11. Rock, A.M., Trainor, L.T. Addison T.L., McMaster University
    Distinctive Messages in Infant-Directed Lullabies and Play Songs
    Developmental Psychology 1999, Vol. 35, No. 2, 527-534.

12. Tamis-LeMonda, C.S., Bornstein, M. H., Braumwill, L., (1989). Maternal Responsiveness and cognitive development in children. New Directions for Child and Adolescent Developments, 49-61.

13. Tamis-LeMonda, C.S., Kuchirko, Y., song, Lulu (2014).
    Why is infant language learning facilitated by parental responsiveness?
    Current Directions of Psychological Science, 23(2) 121-126.

14. Tomasello, M., &, and Farrar, M. J. (1986). Joint attention and early language, Child Development; 57(6) (1986) 1454-1463. Retrieved October 9, 2017 from http://alumni.media.mit.edu/~jorkin/generals/papers/27_tomasello.pdf

15. Wach, T. D. Chan, A., Specificity of environmental action, as seen in environmental correlates of infants' communication performance. Child Development, 57(6), 1464-1474. Retrieved October 9, 2017 from https://www.jstor.org/stable/1130424?orgin=crossref&seq=1#page_scan_tab_contents

Lullabelle & Friends' Parent Diary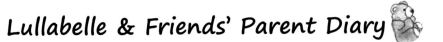

Dear Parents,

This diary can be used to keep track of all the things your baby does when you follow our suggestions!

For example:
#4 - Read to us daily.
   You notice that your baby smiles when she sees the pretty pictures.

OR

You can just keep track of all the exciting, challenging and loving moments that you share with your precious little one from day to day!

Love, Lullabelle, Gabriel, Sydney and Matt

Notes

Notes

Notes

Notes

Notes

Notes

Made in the USA
Middletown, DE
24 September 2020